HAL•LEONARD®

BASS PLAY-ALONG

AUDIO ACCESS INCLUDED

PLAYBACK+
...ed • Pitch • Balance • Loop

Black Sabbath

T0069479

To access audio visit:
www.halleonard.com/mylibrary

5025-0781-9822-8062

Cover photo: © Fin Costello/Redferns/Getty Images

ISBN 978-1-4234-8213-0

HAL•LEONARD®
7777 W. BLUEMOUND RD. P.O. BOX 13819 MILWAUKEE, WI 53213

Visit Hal Leonard Online at
www.halleonard.com

VOL. 26

HAL•LEONARD®
BASS
PLAY-ALONG

AUDIO
ACCESS
INCLUDED

Black Sabbath

CONTENTS

Children of the Grave

Words and Music by Frank Iommi, John Osbourne, William Ward and Terence Butler

Tune down 1 1/2 steps:
(low to high) C#-F#-B-E

Intro
Moderate Rock ♩ = 146

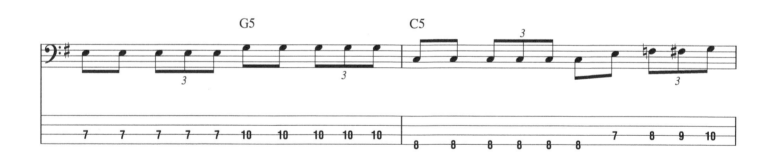

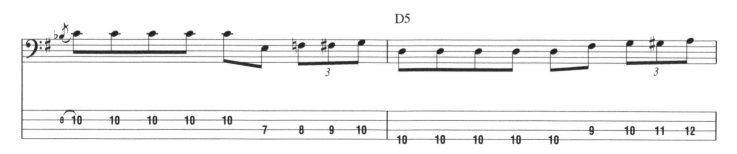

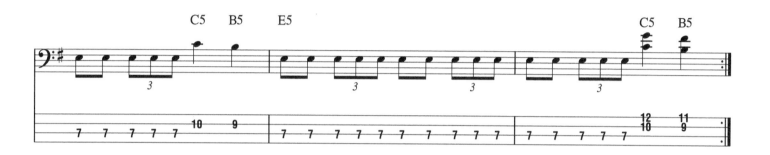

Verse

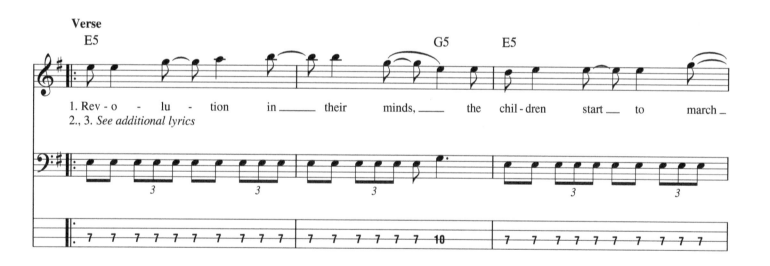

1. Rev - o - lu - tion in ____ their minds, ____ the chil - dren start __ to march __
2., 3. *See additional lyrics*

____ a - gainst the world __ in which they have to live __ in. Oh, the

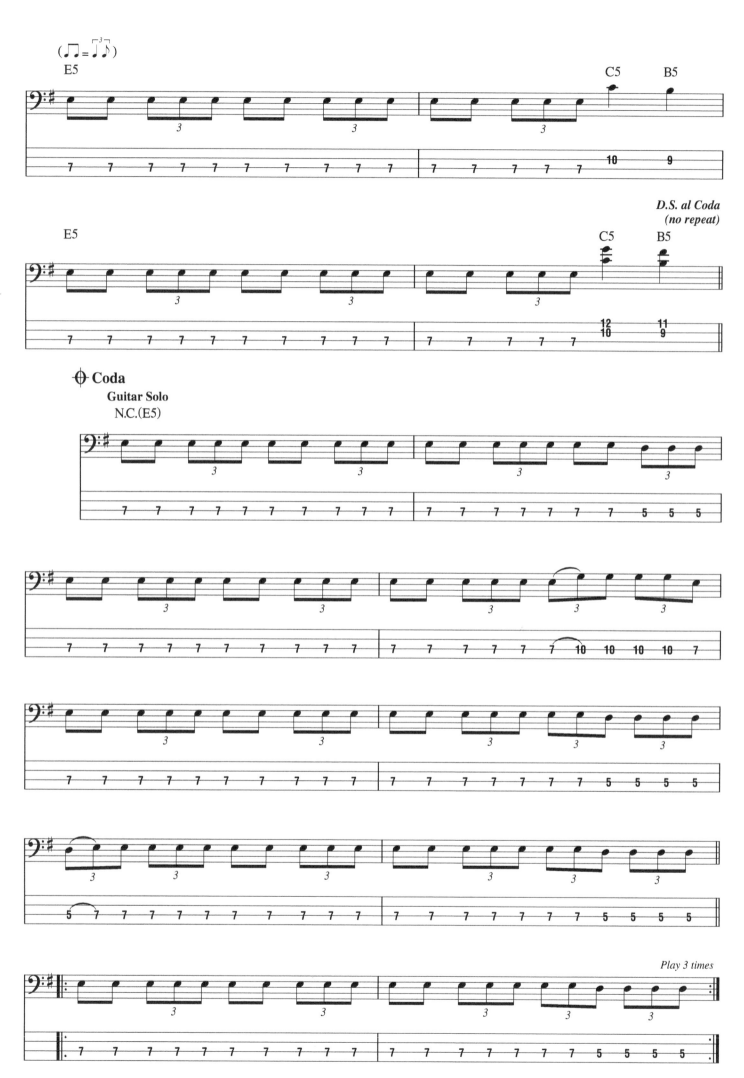

Outro

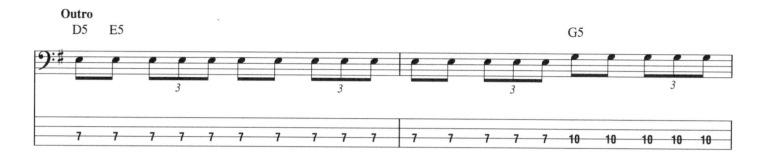

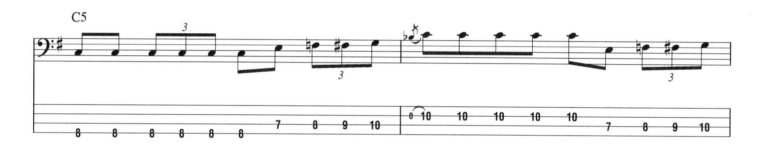

Additional Lyrics

2. Children of tomorrow live
   In the tears that fall today.
   Will the sunrise of tomorrow
   Bring in peace in any way?
   Must the world live
   In the shadow of atomic fear?
   Can they win the fight for peace
   Or will they disappear? Yeah!

3. So, you children of the world,
   Listen to what I say.
   If you want a better place to live in,
   Spread the words today.
   Show the world that love is still alive.
   You must be brave,
   Or you children of today
   Are children of the grave. Yeah!

Iron Man

Words and Music by Frank Iommi, John Osbourne, William Ward and Terence Butler

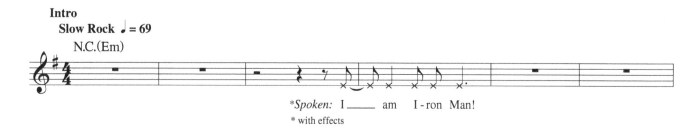

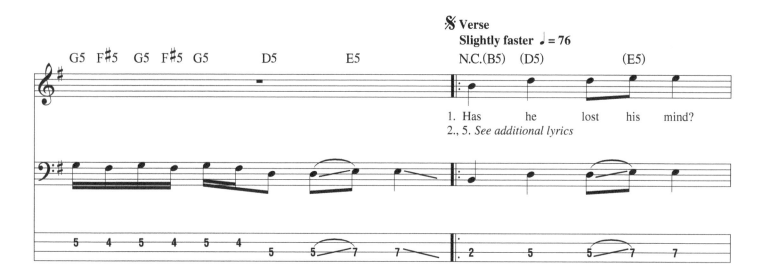

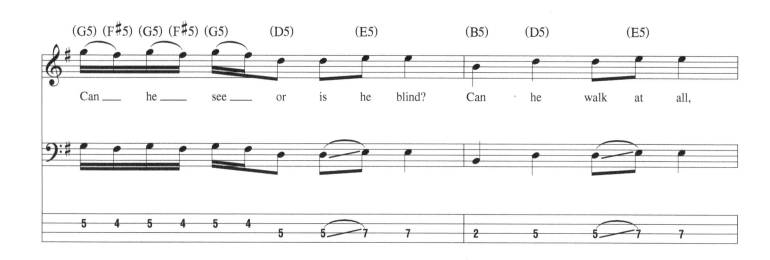

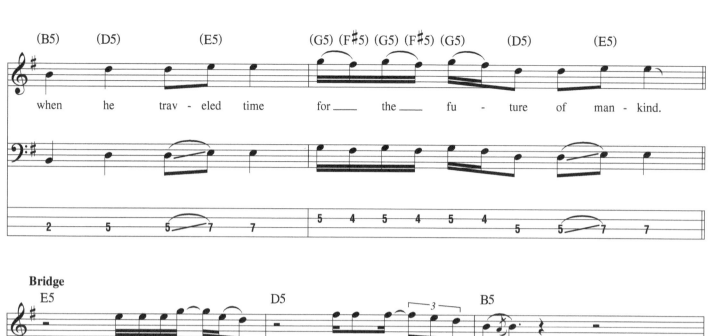

when he trav - eled time for ____ the ____ fu - ture of man - kind.

Bridge

No - bod - y wants _ him, _ he just stares _ at the world. _
See additional lyrics

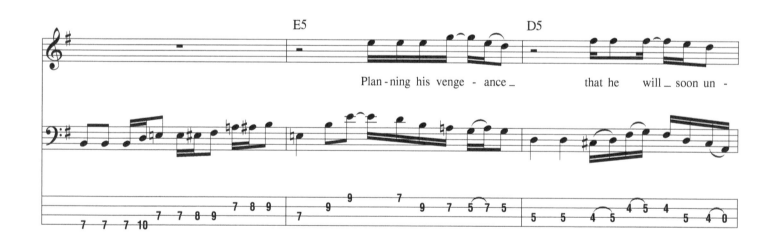

Plan - ning his venge - ance _ that he will _ soon un -

furl. _

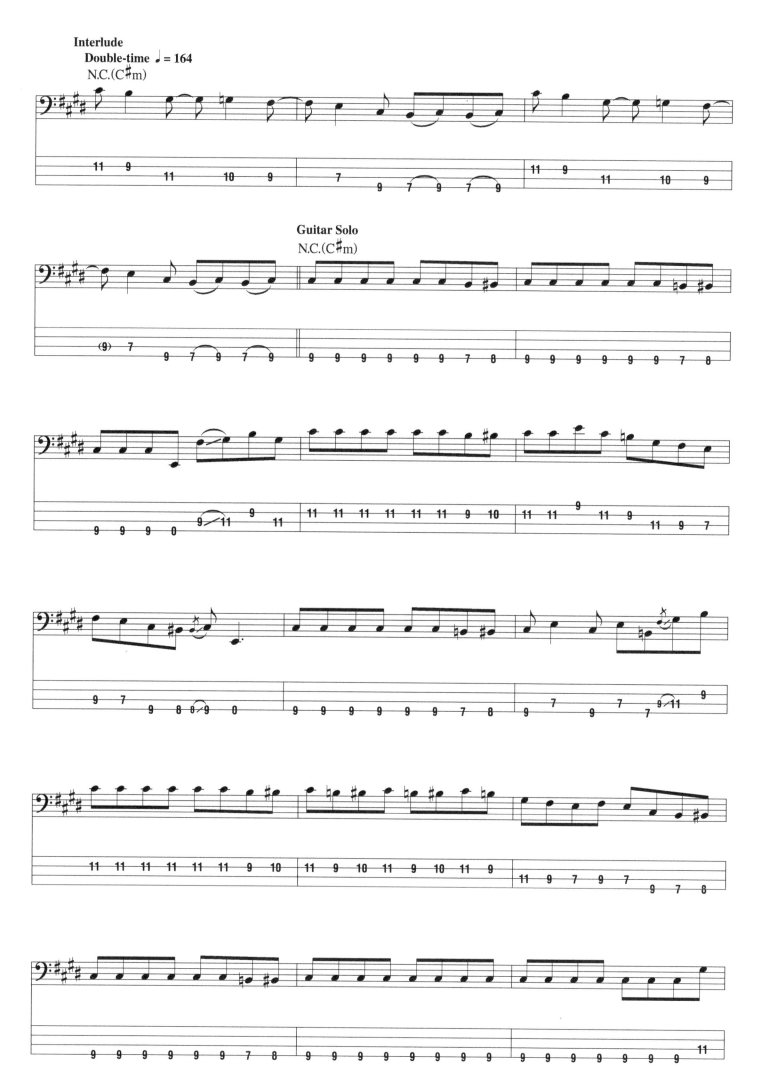

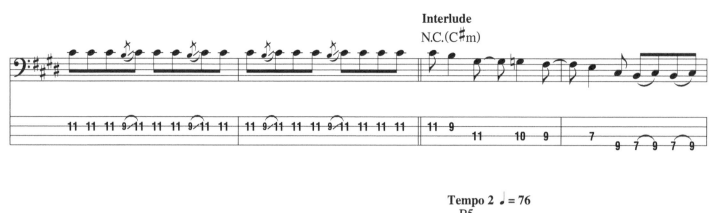

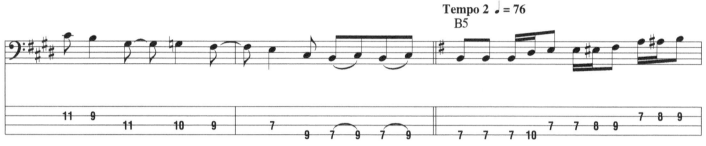

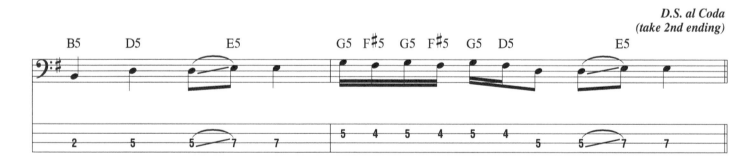

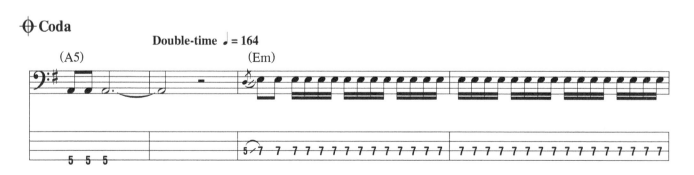

Additional Lyrics

2. Is he live or dead?
   I see thoughts within his head.
   We'll just pass him there.
   Why should we even care?

4. Now the time is here
   For Iron Man to spread fear.
   Vengeance from the grave,
   Kills the people he once saved.

Bridge Nobody wants him,
   They just turn their heads.
   Nobody helps him,
   Now he has revenge.

5. Heavy boots of lead,
   Fills his victims full of dread,
   Running as fast as they can.
   Iron Man lives again!

N.I.B.

Words and Music by Frank Iommi, John Osbourne, William Ward and Terence Butler

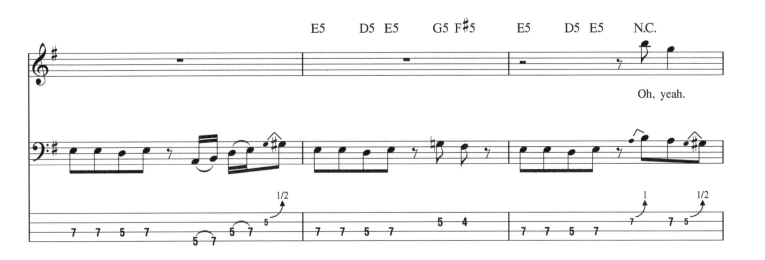

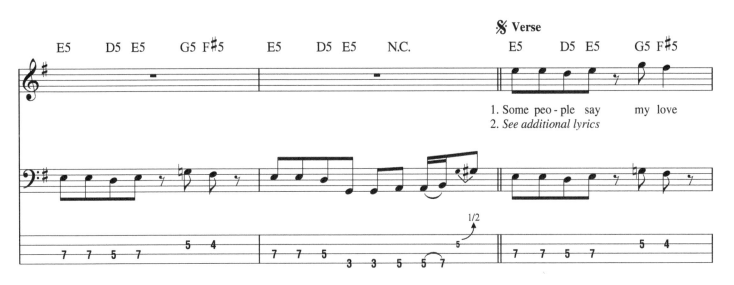

can-not be true. Please be-lieve me, my love, and I'll show you.

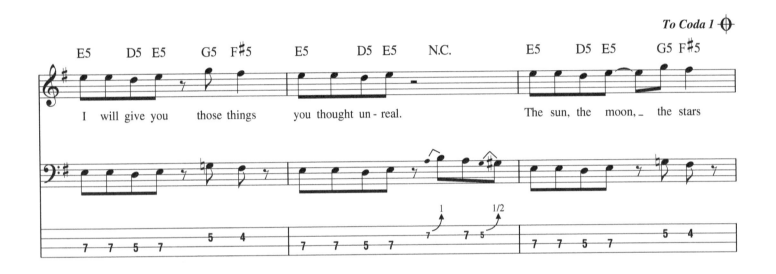

To Coda 1

I will give you those things you thought un-real. The sun, the moon,_ the stars

Interlude

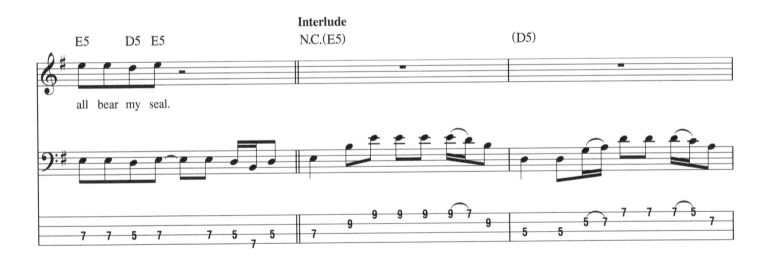

all bear my seal.

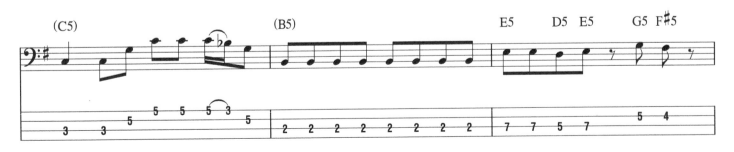

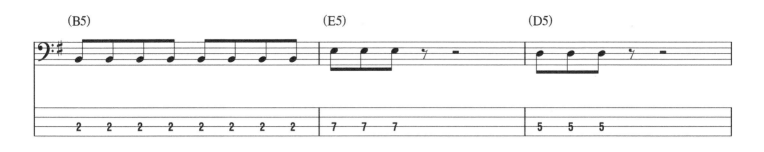

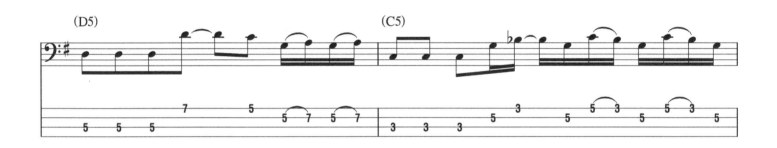

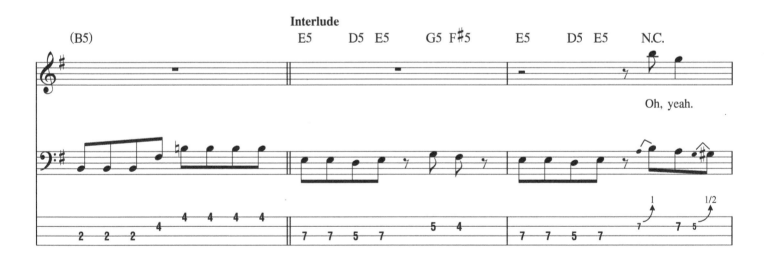

Oh, yeah.

4. Fol-low me now   and you

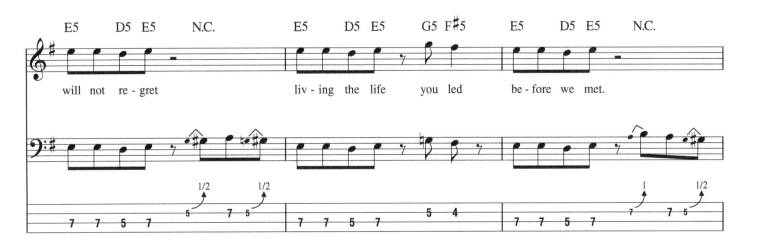

will not re - gret　　　liv - ing the life　you led　　be - fore we met.

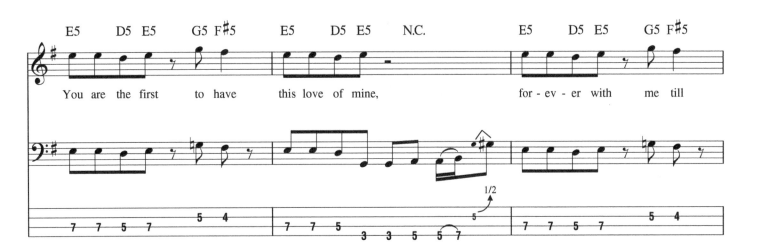

You are the first　　to have　　this love of mine,　　　for - ev - er with　　me till

D.S.S. al Coda 2　　　✛ **Coda 2**

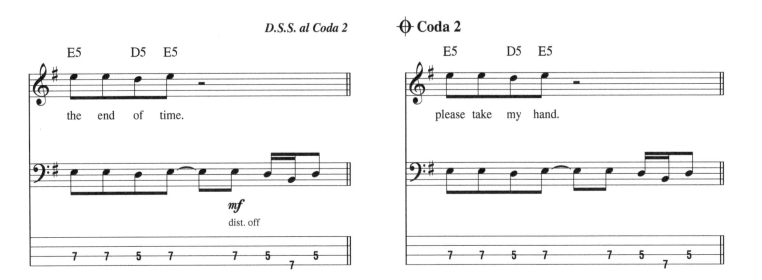

the end of time.　　　　　　　please take　my hand.

Outro

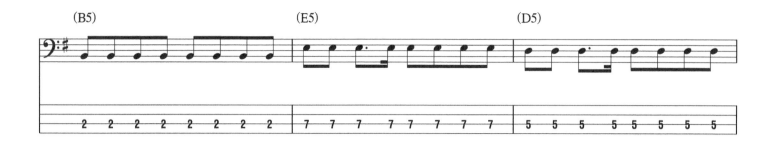

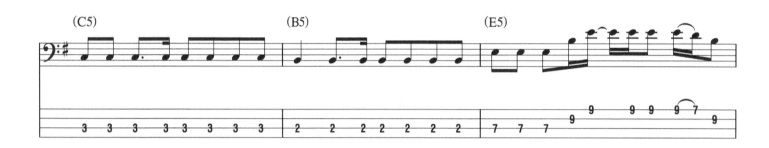

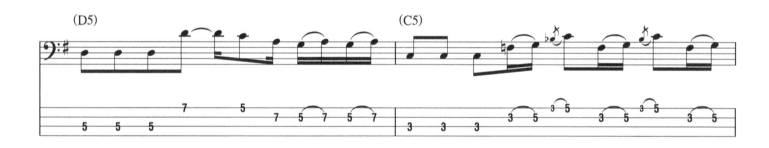

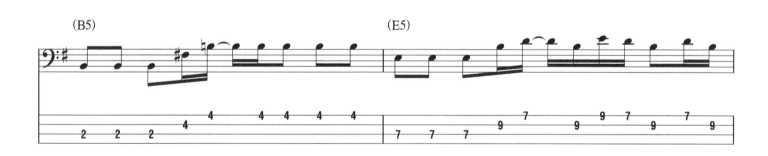

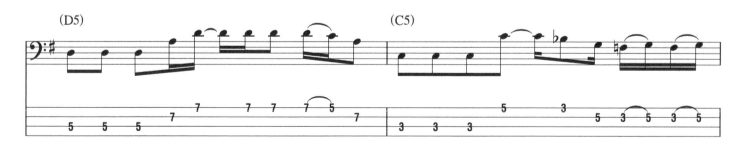

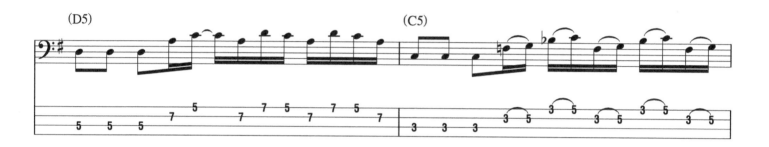

Free time

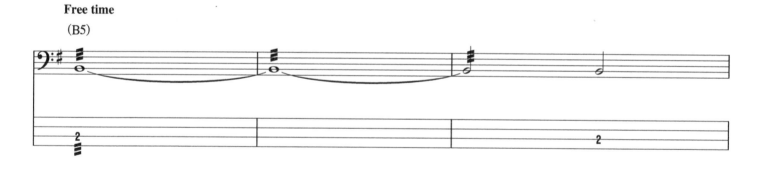

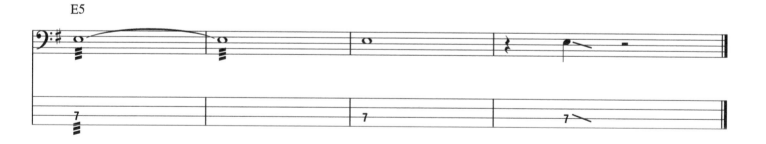

Additional Lyrics

2. Follow me now and you will not regret
Living the life you led before we met.
You are the first to have this love of mine,
Forever with me till the end of time.

Paranoid

Words and Music by Anthony Iommi, John Osbourne, William Ward and Terence Butler

Intro

Fast Rock ♩ = 160

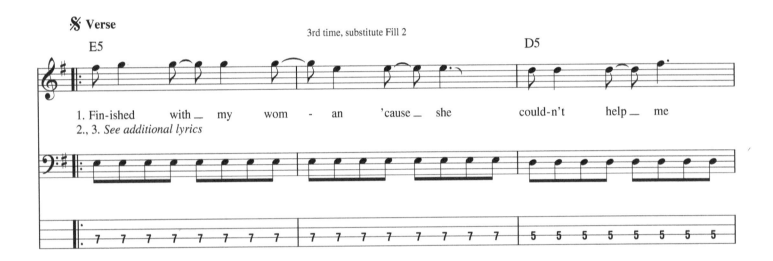

1. Fin-ished with my wom-an 'cause she could-n't help me with my mind.
2., 3. *See additional lyrics*

People think I'm in-sane be-cause I

3rd time, substitute Fill 2

2nd time, substitute Fill 1
3rd time, substitute Fill 2

Whoa, _____ yeah! _____

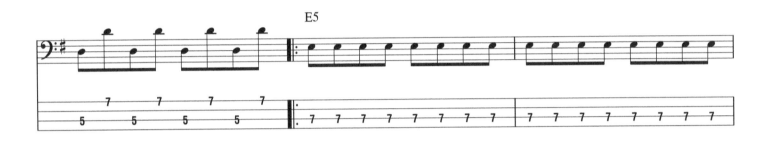

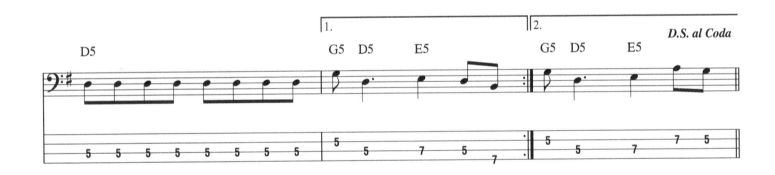

1.

2.

D.S. al Coda

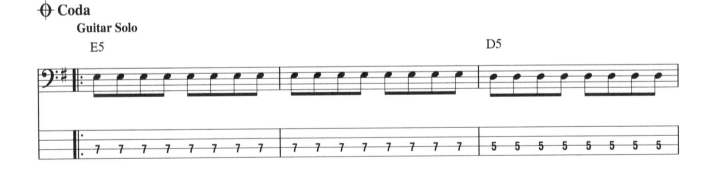

⊕ **Coda**

Guitar Solo

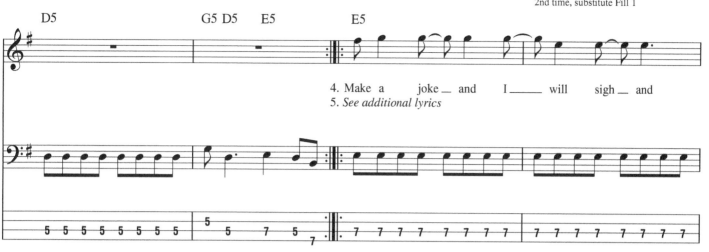

4. Make a joke __ and I ____ will sigh __ and
5. *See additional lyrics*

you will laugh __ and I ____ will cry. Hap - pi - ness __ a - gain __

2nd time, substitute Fill 1

__ I feel __ and love to me __ is so un - real.

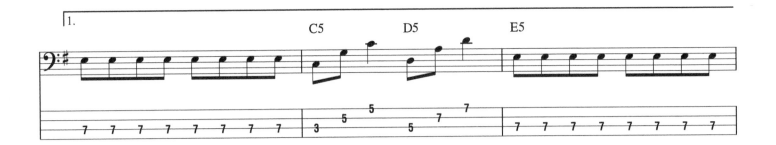

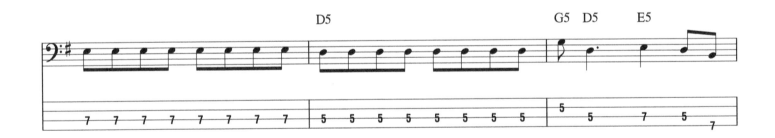

Additional Lyrics

2. All day long I think of things but nothing seems to satisfy.
   Think I'll lose my mind if I don't find something to pacify.

3. I need someone to show me the things in life that I can't find.
   I can't see the things that make true happiness; I must be blind.

5. And so as you hear these words telling you now of my state.
   I tell you to enjoy life, I wish I could but it's too late.

Sabbath, Bloody Sabbath

Words and Music by Frank Iommi, John Osbourne, William Ward and Terence Butler

Tune down 1 1/2 steps:
(low to high) C#-F#-B-E

Intro

Moderately slow Rock ♩ = 66

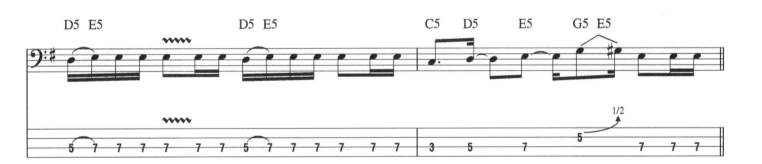

1. You see right through dis-tort-ed eyes, ____ you know you have to ____ learn. ____
2. *See additional lyrics*

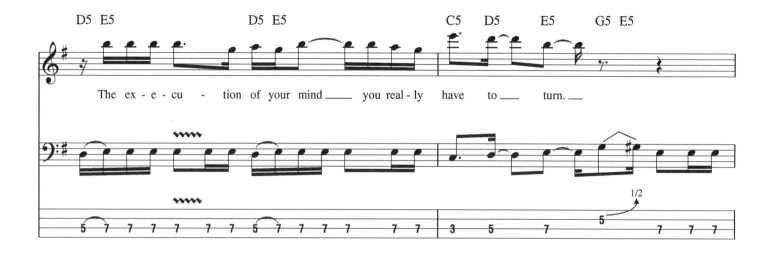

The ex - e - cu - tion of your mind ____ you real - ly have to ____ turn. ____

2nd time, substitute Fill 1

The race is run, the book is read, the end be - gins to ____ show. ____

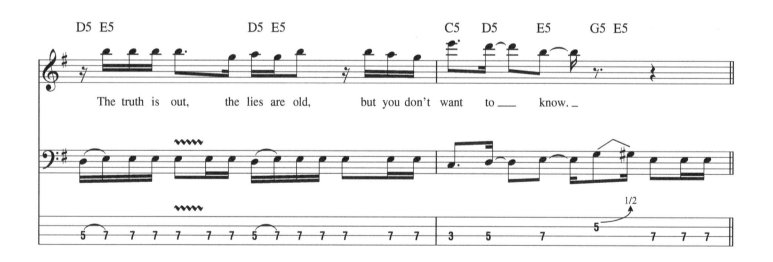

The truth is out, the lies are old, but you don't want to ____ know. ____

Fill 1

Interlude

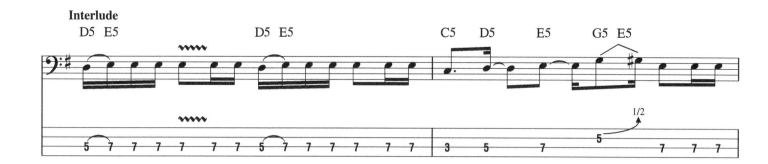

D.S. al Coda

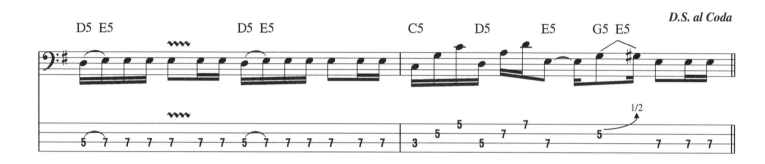

Coda

You   bas - tards!

Guitar Solo

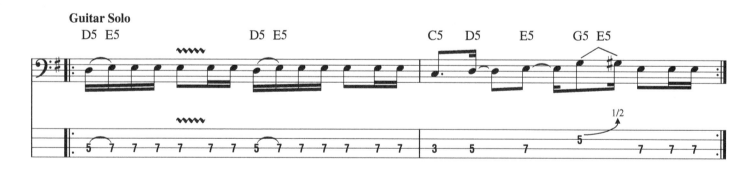

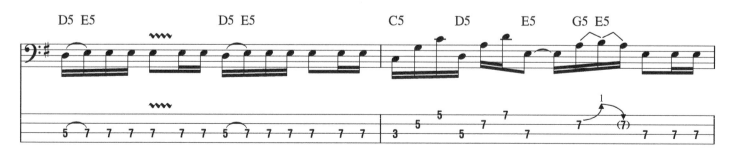

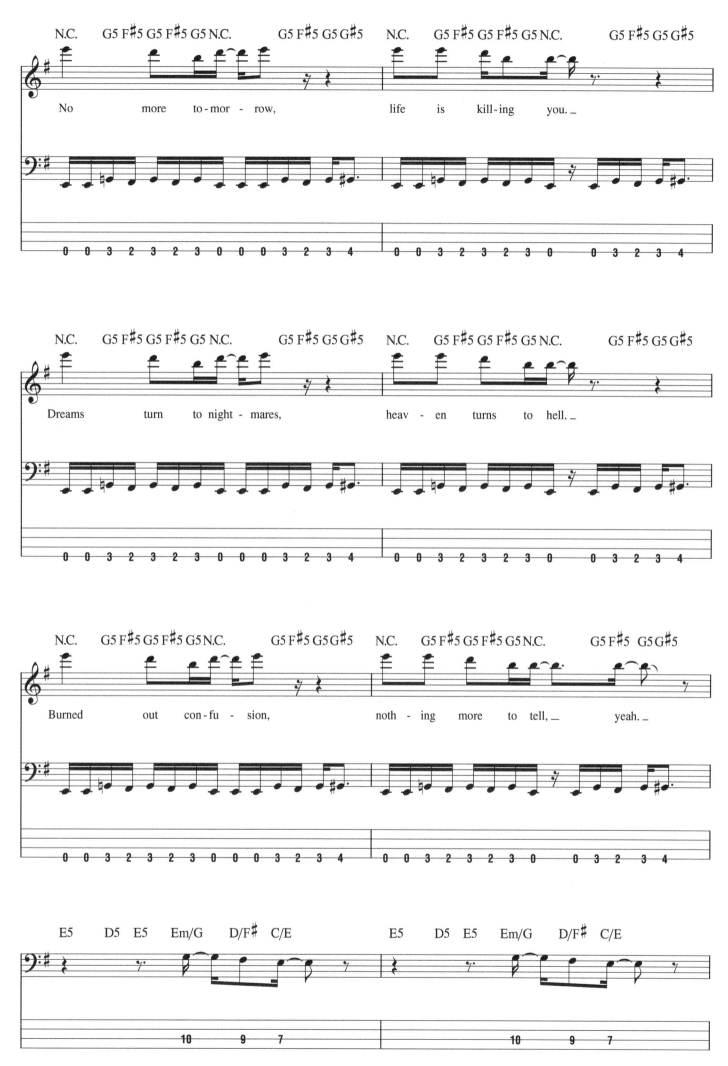

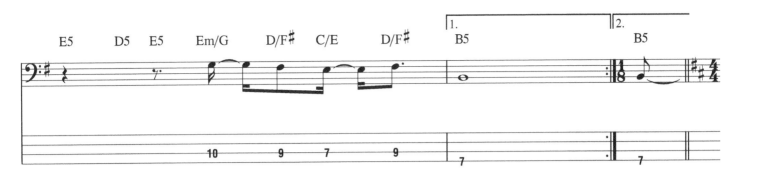

Outro
Double-time feel

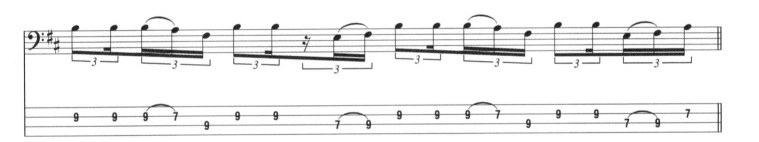

Repeat and fade

Additional Lyrics

2. The people who have crippled you,
   You wanna see them burn.
   The gates of life have closed on you
   And there's just no return.
   You're wishing that the hands of doom
   Could take your mind away,
   And you don't care if you don't see
   Again the light of day.

Bridge Ev'rything around you, what's it coming to?
   God knows as your dog knows,
   Bog blast all of you.
   Sabbath, bloody Sabbath,
   Nothing more to do.
   Living just for dying,
   Dying just for you, yeah.

Sweet Leaf

Words and Music by Frank Iommi, John Osbourne, William Ward and Terence Butler

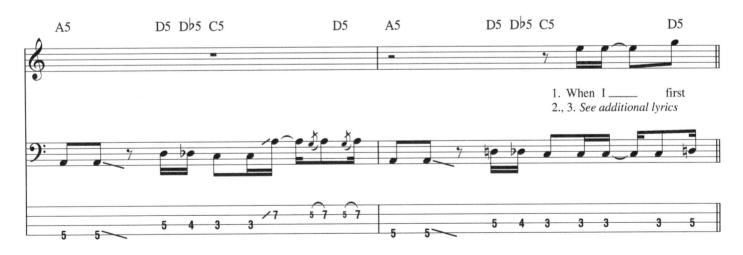

Interlude

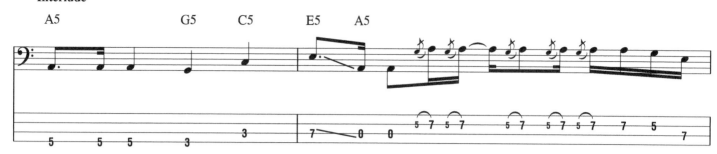

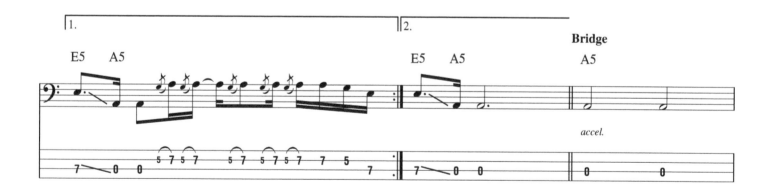

Guitar Solo

N.C.

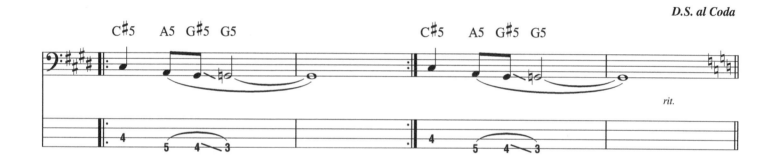

D.S. al Coda

Additional Lyrics

2. My life was empty, forever on a down.
   Until you took me, showed me around.
   My life is free now, my life is clear.
   I love you sweet leaf, though you can't hear.

3. Straight people don't know what you're about.
   They put you down and shut you out.
   You gave to me a new belief.
   And soon the world will love you, sweet leaf.

War Pigs
(Interpolating Luke's Wall)

Words and Music by Frank Iommi, John Osbourne, William Ward and Terence Butler

Pre-Intro
Slow Rock ♩ = 56

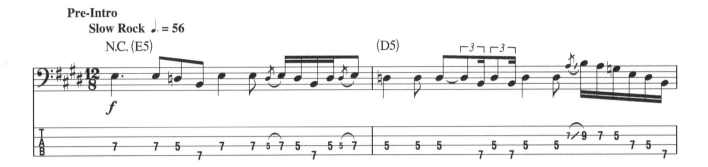

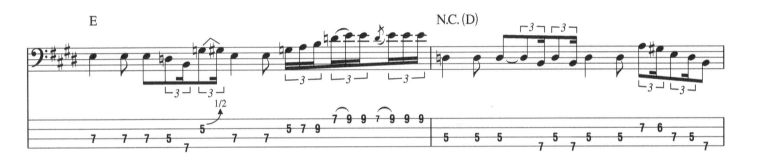

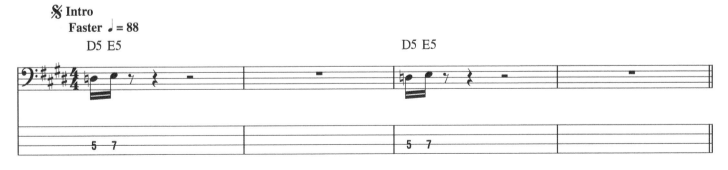

§ Intro
Faster ♩ = 88

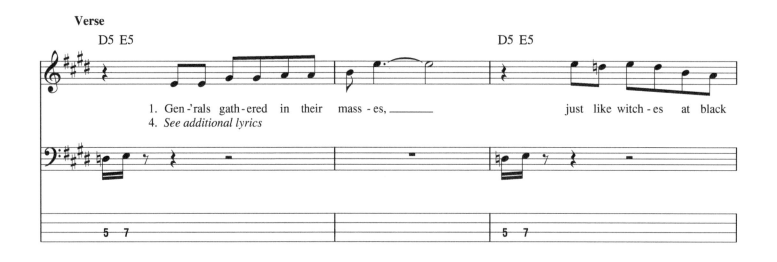

1. Gen-'rals gath-ered in their mass-es, _____ just like witch-es at black
4. *See additional lyrics*

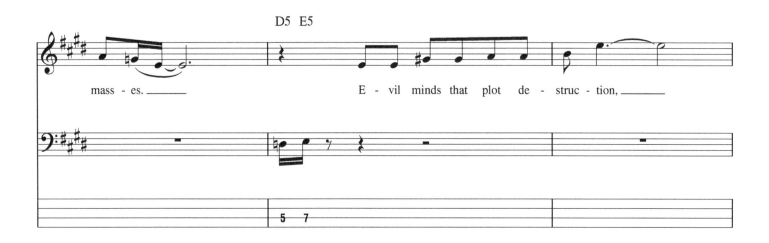

mass - es. _____ E - vil minds that plot de - struc - tion, _____

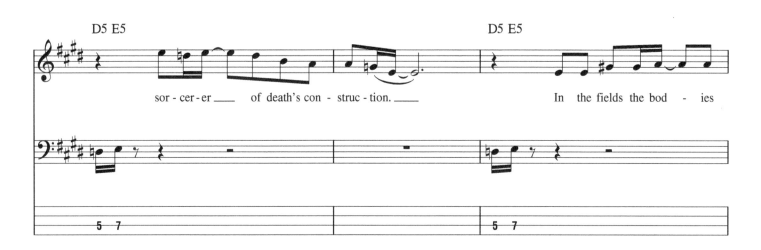

sor - cer - er _____ of death's con - struc - tion. _____ In the fields the bod - ies

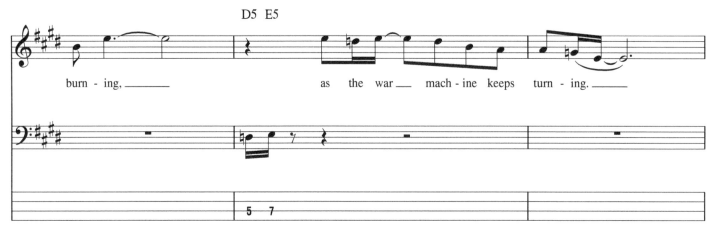

burn - ing, _____ as the war ____ mach - ine keeps turn - ing. _____

Death and ha - tred to man - kind, _____ pois - on - ing ___ their brain-washed

Interlude

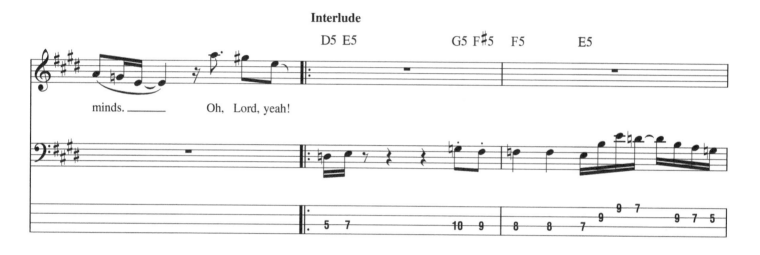

minds. _____ Oh, Lord, yeah!

4th time, To Coda

Verse

2nd time, substitute Fill 1

N.C. (E5)

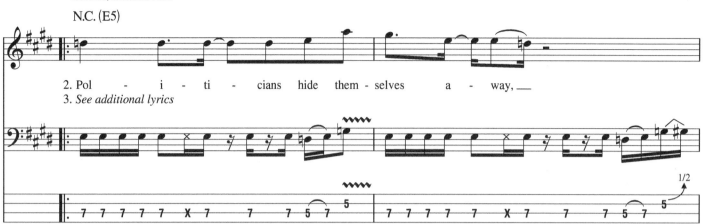

2. Pol - i - ti - cians hide them - selves   a - way, ___
3. *See additional lyrics*

they   on - ly start - ed   the ___ war. _____

Fill 1

Why should they   go out   to   fight?

They   leave   that   all   to   the   poor!   Yeah!

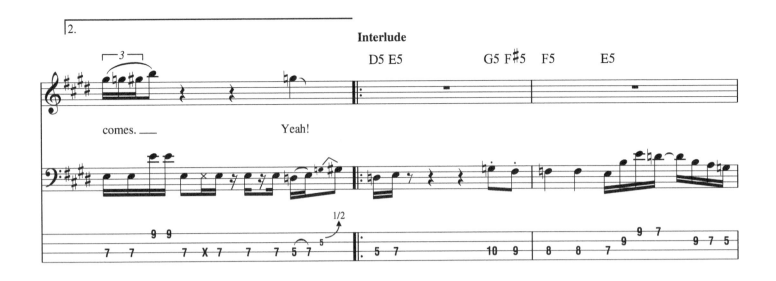

Interlude

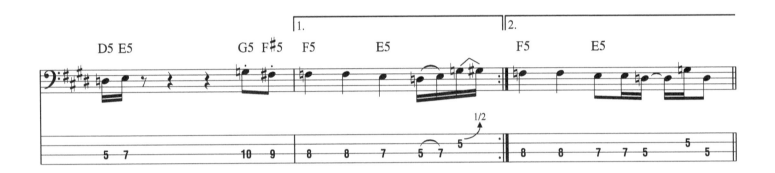

Guitar Solo

N.C. (E5)

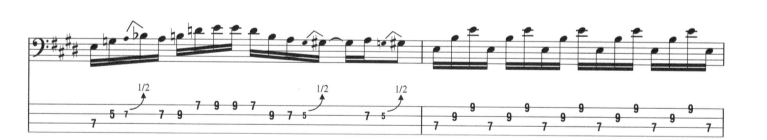

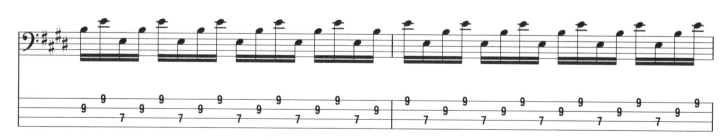

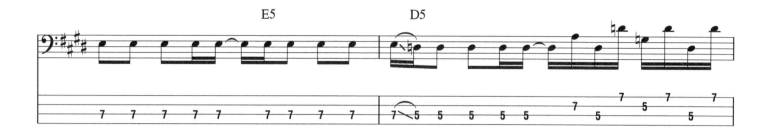

D.S. al Coda
(take repeat)

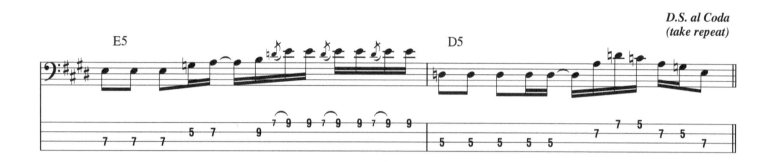

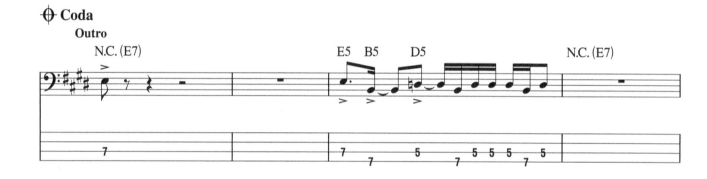

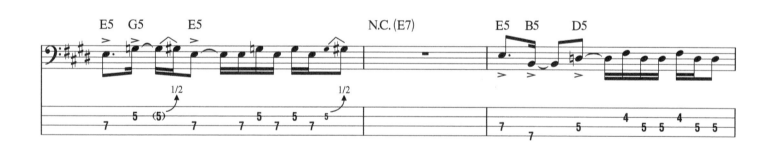

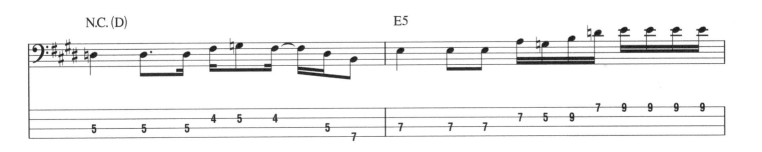

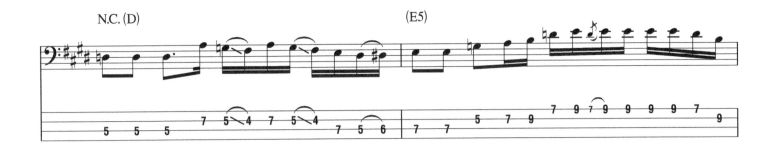

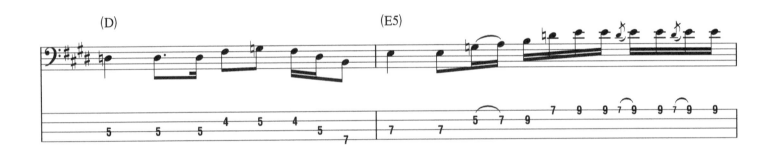

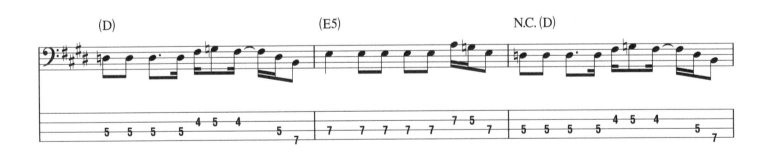

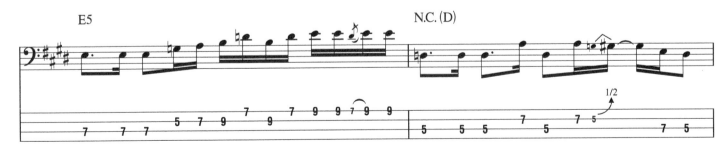

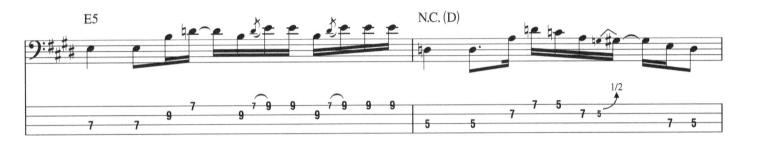

*Tape speeds up; last note sounds 10 ½ steps higher.

Additional Lyrics

3. Time will tell on their power minds,
   Making war just for fun.
   Treating people just like pawns in chess,
   Wait till their judgment day comes. Yeah!

4. Now in darkness, world stops turning,
   Ashes where the bodies burning.
   No more war pigs have the power.
   Hand of God has struck the hour.
   Day of judgment, God is calling,
   On their knees, the war pigs crawling.
   Begging mercies for their sins,
   Satan laughing, spreads his wings.
   Oh, Lord, yeah!

Bass Notation Legend

Bass music can be notated two different ways: on a *musical staff*, and in *tablature*

THE MUSICAL STAFF shows pitches and rhythms and is divided by bar lines into measures. Pitches are named after the first seven letters of the alphabet.

TABLATURE graphically represents the bass fingerboard. Each horizontal line represents a string, and each number represents a fret.

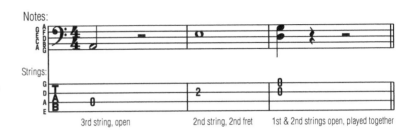

3rd string, open   2nd string, 2nd fret   1st & 2nd strings open, played together

HAMMER-ON: Strike the first (lower) note with one finger, then sound the higher note (on the same string) with another finger by fretting it without picking.

PULL-OFF: Place both fingers on the notes to be sounded. Strike the first note and without picking, pull the finger off to sound the second (lower) note.

LEGATO SLIDE: Strike the first note and then slide the same fret-hand finger up or down to the second note. The second note is not struck.

SHIFT SLIDE: Same as legato slide, except the second note is struck.

TRILL: Very rapidly alternate between the notes indicated by continuously hammering on and pulling off.

TREMOLO PICKING: The note is picked as rapidly and continuously as possible.

VIBRATO: The string is vibrated by rapidly bending and releasing the note with the fretting hand.

SHAKE: Using one finger, rapidly alternate between two notes on one string by sliding either a half-step above or below.

NATURAL HARMONIC: Strike the note while the fret hand lightly touches the string directly over the fret indicated.

MUFFLED STRINGS: A percussive sound is produced by laying the fret hand across the string(s) without depressing them and striking them with the pick hand.

BEND: Strike the note and bend up the interval shown.

BEND AND RELEASE: Strike the note and bend up as indicated, then release back to the original note. Only the first note is struck.

RIGHT-HAND TAP: Hammer ("tap") the fret indicated with the "pick-hand" index or middle finger and pull off to the note fretted by the fret hand.

LEFT-HAND TAP: Hammer ("tap") the fret indicated with the "fret-hand" index or middle finger.

SLAP: Strike ("slap") string with right-hand thumb.

POP: Snap ("pop") string with right-hand index or middle finger.

Additional Musical Definitions

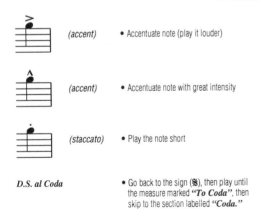

(accent) • Accentuate note (play it louder)

(accent) • Accentuate note with great intensity

(staccato) • Play the note short

D.S. al Coda • Go back to the sign (𝄋), then play until the measure marked ***"To Coda"***, then skip to the section labelled ***"Coda."***

Fill • Label used to identify a brief pattern which is to be inserted into the arrangement.

• Repeat measures between signs.

• When a repeated section has different endings, play the first ending only the first time and the second ending only the second time.

54

HAL•LEONARD®
BASS
PLAY-ALONG

The Bass Play-Along™ Series will help you play your favorite songs quickly and easily! Just follow the tab, listen to the audio to hear how the bass should sound, and then play-along using the separate backing tracks. The melody and lyrics are also included in the book in case you want to sing, or to simply help you follow along. The audio files are enhanced so you can adjust the recording to any tempo without changing pitch!

1. Rock
00699674 Book/Online Audio $16.99

2. R&B
00699675 Book/Online Audio $16.99

3. Songs for Beginners
00346426 Book/Online Audio $16.99

4. '90s Rock
00294992 Book/Online Audio $16.99

5. Funk
00699680 Book/Online Audio $16.99

6. Classic Rock
00699678 Book/Online Audio $17.99

8. Punk Rock
00699813 Book/CD Pack $12.95

9. Blues
00699817 Book/Online Audio.................................$16.99

10. Jimi Hendrix – Smash Hits
00699815 Book/Online Audio.................................$17.99

11. Country
00699818 Book/CD Pack $12.95

12. Punk Classics
00699814 Book/CD Pack $12.99

13. The Beatles
00275504 Book/Online Audio $17.99

14. Modern Rock
00699821 Book/CD Pack......................................$14.99

15. Mainstream Rock
00699822 Book/CD Pack......................................$14.99

16. '80s Metal
00699825 Book/CD Pack......................................$16.99

17. Pop Metal
00699826 Book/CD Pack......................................$14.99

18. Blues Rock
00699828 Book/CD Pack......................................$19.99

19. Steely Dan
00700203 Book/Online Audio $17.99

20. The Police
00700270 Book/Online Audio $19.99

21. Metallica: 1983-1988
00234338 Book/Online Audio $19.99

22. Metallica: 1991-2016
00234339 Book/Online Audio $19.99

23. Pink Floyd – Dark Side of The Moon
00700847 Book/Online Audio $16.99

24. Weezer
00700960 Book/CD Pack $17.99

25. Nirvana
00701047 Book/Online Audio $17.99

26. Black Sabbath
00701180 Book/Online Audio $17.99

27. Kiss
00701181 Book/Online Audio.................................$17.99

28. The Who
00701182 Book/Online Audio $19.99

29. Eric Clapton
00701183 Book/Online Audio $17.99

30. Early Rock
00701184 Book/CD Pack.....................................$15.99

31. The 1970s
00701185 Book/CD Pack.....................................$14.99

32. Cover Band Hits
00211598 Book/Online Audio $16.99

33. Christmas Hits
00701197 Book/CD Pack.....................................$12.99

34. Easy Songs
00701480 Book/Online Audio $17.99

35. Bob Marley
00701702 Book/Online Audio $17.99

36. Aerosmith
00701886 Book/CD Pack.....................................$14.99

37. Modern Worship
00701920 Book/Online Audio $19.99

38. Avenged Sevenfold
00702386 Book/CD Pack.....................................$16.99

39. Queen
00702387 Book/Online Audio $17.99

40. AC/DC
14041594 Book/Online Audio $17.99

41. U2
00702582 Book/Online Audio $19.99

42. Red Hot Chili Peppers
00702991 Book/Online Audio.................................$19.99

43. Paul McCartney
00703079 Book/Online Audio.................................$19.99

44. Megadeth
00703080 Book/CD Pack.....................................$16.99

45. Slipknot
00703201 Book/CD Pack $17.99

46. Best Bass Lines Ever
00103359 Book/Online Audio.................................$19.99

47. Dream Theater
00111940 Book/Online Audio $24.99

48. James Brown
00117421 Book/CD Pack.....................................$16.99

49. Eagles
00119936 Book/Online Audio.................................$17.99

50. Jaco Pastorius
00128407 Book/Online Audio $17.99

51. Stevie Ray Vaughan
00146154 Book/CD Pack.....................................$16.99

52. Cream
00146159 Book/Online Audio $19.99

56. Bob Seger
00275503 Book/Online Audio.................................$16.99

57. Iron Maiden
00278398 Book/Online Audio $17.99

58. Southern Rock
00278436 Book/Online Audio $17.99

HAL•LEONARD®

Prices, contents, and availability subject to change without notice.

Visit Hal Leonard Online at **www.halleonard.com**

BASS RECORDED VERSIONS

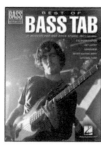

Bass Recorded Versions feature authentic transcriptions written in standard notation and tablature for bass guitar. This series features complete bass lines from the classics to contemporary superstars.

25 Essential Rock Bass Classics
00690210 / $19.99

Avenged Sevenfold – Nightmare
00691054 / $19.99

The Beatles – Abbey Road
00128336 / $24.99

The Beatles – 1962-1966
00690556 / $19.99

The Beatles – 1967-1970
00690557 / $24.99

Best of Bass Tab
00141806 / $17.99

The Best of Blink 182
00690549 / $18.99

Blues Bass Classics
00690291 / $22.99

Boston – Bass Collection
00690935 / $19.95

Stanley Clarke – Collection
00672307 / $22.99

Dream Theater – Bass Anthology
00119345 / $29.99

Funk Bass Bible
00690744 / $27.99

Hard Rock Bass Bible
00690746 / $22.99

**Jimi Hendrix –
Are You Experienced?**
00690371 / $17.95

Jimi Hendrix – Bass Tab Collection
00160505 / $24.99

Iron Maiden – Bass Anthology
00690867 / $24.99

Jazz Bass Classics
00102070 / $19.99

The Best of Kiss
00690080 / $22.99

**Lynyrd Skynyrd –
All-Time Greatest Hits**
00690956 / $24.99

Bob Marley – Bass Collection
00690568 / $24.99

Mastodon – Crack the Skye
00691007 / $19.99

Megadeth – Bass Anthology
00691191 / $22.99

Metal Bass Tabs
00103358 / $22.99

Best of Marcus Miller
00690811 / $29.99

Motown Bass Classics
00690253 / $19.99

Muse – Bass Tab Collection
00123275 / $22.99

Nirvana – Bass Collection
00690066 / $19.99

**Nothing More –
Guitar & Bass Collection**
00265439 / $24.99

The Offspring – Greatest Hits
00690809 / $17.95

The Essential Jaco Pastorius
00690420 / $22.99

**Jaco Pastorius –
Greatest Jazz Fusion Bass Player**
00690421 / $24.99

Pearl Jam – Ten
00694882 / $22.99

Pink Floyd – Dark Side of the Moon
00660172 / $19.99

The Best of Police
00660207 / $24.99

Pop/Rock Bass Bible
00690747 / $24.99

Queen – The Bass Collection
00690065 / $22.99

R&B Bass Bible
00690745 / $24.99

Rage Against the Machine
00690248 / $22.99

**Red Hot Chili Peppers –
BloodSugarSexMagik**
00690064 / $22.99

**Red Hot Chili Peppers –
By the Way**
00690585 / $24.99

**Red Hot Chili Peppers –
Californication**
00690390 / $22.99

**Red Hot Chili Peppers –
Greatest Hits**
00690675 / $22.99

**Red Hot Chili Peppers –
I'm with You**
00691167 / $22.99

**Red Hot Chili Peppers –
One Hot Minute**
00690091 / $22.99

**Red Hot Chili Peppers –
Stadium Arcadium**
00690853 / Book Only $24.95

Rock Bass Bible
00690446 / $22.99

Rolling Stones – Bass Collection
00690256 / $24.99

Royal Blood
00151826 / $24.99

**Rush – The Spirit of Radio:
Greatest Hits 1974-1987**
00323856 / $24.99

Best of Billy Sheehan
00173972 / $24.99

Slap Bass Bible
00159716 / $29.99

Sly & The Family Stone for Bass
00109733 / $24.99

Best of Yes
00103044 / $24.99

Best of ZZ Top for Bass
00691069 / $24.99